THE BIRTHING OF A CHURCH

LEROY NEWMAN

Copyright © 2020 by Leroy Newman.

ISBN   Softcover   978-1-953537-24-9

All rights reserved. No part of this book may be reproduced or transmitted in any form or by any means, electronic or mechanical, including photocopying, recording, or by any information storage and retrieval system without express written permission from the author, except in the case of brief quotations embodied in critical reviews and certain other non-commercial uses permitted by copyright law.

Unless otherwise indicated, all scripture quotations in this book are from the
    King James Version of the Bible.
Bibles: New International Version
          New King James Version
          American Standard Bible

Printed in the United States of America.

To order additional copies of this book, contact:
Bookwhip
1-855-339-3589
https://www.bookwhip.com

TIME MINISTRY BOOK
&
Troy 4 Life Production

Time Ministry Books
115-11 229th Street, Cambria Heights, NY 11411
1 718 723-3716

CONTENTS

Foreword 1
Acknowledgments 3
Introduction 5
The Birthing of a Church 7
The Birth of a Church 13
The Servant's Heart 19
The Theocracy of the Church 21
Love and Discipleship 26
Why the Church Must be Organized 29
Leadership that Hinders the Move of God 31
Vision 34

Part Two

The Underrower 39
Ture Servants of Christ 43
Servant Leadership 48
The Visionary and the Servant 51
The Disposition of the Underrower 52
Availability 55
The Sacrifice 59
Visionary Purpose 61
From Current Reality to Visionary Purpose 64
Prayers of the Underrower 67
The Weapon of our Warfare 70

FOREWORD

The Birthing of the Church is the work of our Chief Apostle, Bishop Leroy C. E. Newman; it is meant to strengthen the fellowship and promote community outreach; I thank God for his vision and the visionary purpose of those under his oversight. This ministry is committed to the teaching of the Gospel of Jesus Church and the saving of souls.

This Church is an inner-city ministry with an outreach that focuses on family-structure, community involvement, spiritual commitment, educational achievement, and economical enrichment. The members of this ministry have served this community for decades. It has a rewarding educational assistance and tutorial programs and continues to aid in the personal development of its members and church leaders.

This Church is first and foremost committed to the spiritual development of the its members and the members of the community who commit to the teaching of Jesus Christ as outlined in the Holy Bible. It is also committed to the social and economic development of the community in which it serves. It will assist its community by offering educational opportunity to its members, to whom, in most cases, an unacceptable level of educational opportunities and services have traditionally been below national standards. We take great pride in defying the odds, offering hope and providing a real chance for success spiritually, socially, and economically to all who come to it for assistance.

ACKNOWLEDGMENTS

The Pulpit Commentary:
    Edited by H.D. Spence and Joseph S. Exell,
    Volumes 1-22; Wm. B. Eerdmans
    Publishing Company, Grand Rapids, Michigan

PC Bible:
    Mathew Henry's commentary
    Kell and Delitzsch on the Old Testament

Strategic Thinking for the '90s
    The Pacific Institute

Hebrews – Better things:
    Volume 1 - Daniel Seagraves

World aflame Adult Teacher's:
    Pentecostal Publishing House

INTRODUCTION

THE BIRTHING OF THE CHURCH

"The Underrower"

Many of those who have read this book read it because of their relationship with a friend who recommended it or because of their relationship with me or a Pastor over which I have oversight.

No matter for what reason they have for reading it, I am convinced that it will change the way they see the Church. The one thing I hope to do as you read this book is to change the way you think about church leadership.

It is said, "There is nothing good or bad, but thinking makes it so." The truth is, "As a man thinketh, so is he, Proverb 23:7.

We are all created in this world with a purpose whether we go to church of not; the key to fulfillment and stepping into your purpose is your faith and trust in God. Purpose has nothing to do with the physical, for in it there is no spiritual value. When we trust in the arms of the flesh, we deceive ourselves and deny ourselves of the riches of God Graces.

Paul admonishes us to "Trust in the Lord, and lean not unto your own understanding but in all our ways acknowledge Him (God) and He shall direct our path (your will, your going in and coming out) *Proverbs 3:5-6*.

In Proverbs 3, the preacher is saying to every believer, although there is much to be gained by embracing natural wisdom, we must not lean to our own understanding, or self-sufficiency, or self-dependence or even our own self-sacrificing; that which is more beneficial in our walk with God is our devotion and our total reliance on Him and our patient submissiveness to His Divine Will for us.

THE BIRTHING OF A CHURCH

"The Underrowers"

The Church is an inner-city ministry with an outreach that focuses on love, family structure, community support and involvement, spiritual commitment, educational achievement, and economical enrichment. Most ministries have served the same community for years. Some have rewarding educational assistance and tutorial programs and continues to aid in the personal development of community members and church leaders.

The Church is first and foremost committed to the spiritual development of the its members and the members of the community who commit to the teaching of Jesus Christ as outlined in the Holy Bible. It is also committed to the social and economic development of the community in which it serves. It assists its community by offering educational opportunity to its members, to whom, in most cases, an unacceptable level of educational opportunities and services have traditionally been below national standards. The Church should take great pride in defying the odds, offering hope, and providing a real chance for success, spiritually, socially, and economically to all who come to it for assistance.

The church

> *And without controversy great is the mystery of godliness: God was manifest in the flesh, justified in the Spirit, seen of angels, preached unto the Gentiles, believed on in the world, received up into glory.*
>
> I Timothy 3:16

The spiritual development of a congregation depends largely upon the spiritual character of those who minister to it; the choice of fit ministers to serve in the sacred ministry of God's Church is a matter of vital importance to the welfare of the people, and demands the utmost wisdom and trustworthiness of those who have the chief oversight of the house of God. Its pastor must have an irreproachable character both secular and spiritual (among those inside the fellowship and those outside of the ministry).

The character and countenance of the leaders of the church must not give way to a lax morality, but command strict temperance, a staid sober mind and demeanor; besides these strictly personal qualifications, church leaders must have well-ordered households, especially the pastors. Their families must bear the traces of a gentle but firm parental discipline. They that are rulers in the house of God must show that they can rule their own children and servants; a portion of the gravity and sobriety of the leaders in God's house should be seen in the members of their household; this is not to say that the leader's children must be perfect or that they should even attend church at all. The scripture says the leader must rule his house; this means that he sets the order in his house as an example to other families.

The church is an institution of order. Paul writes to Timothy, "These things I write to thee, hoping to come shortly; but if I should tarry, [I write them] *that thou mayest know how thou ought to conduct thyself in God's house.*" It was not enough for Timothy to stir up his own personal gifts and do the work of an evangelist, but he must execute the special commission he had received from the apostle, to regulate the appointment of the office bearers of the Church and the details of Church worship. A minister should always look more to his calling as a visionary than to the honor and advantage that comes with his appointment

What is the church?

Is the church a building? Is it the place where believers gather to worship? Or is the church the people—the believers who follow Christ? How we understand and perceive the church is quite important in determining how we live out our faith.

The church in the new testament

For the purpose of this study, we will look at the idea of "THE CHURCH" in the context of "The Christian Church," which is the New Testament concept of the Church.

Jesus was the first to mention the church: Simon Peter replied, "You are the Christ, the Son of the living God." And Jesus answered him, 'Blessed are you, Simon Bar-Jonah,' for flesh and blood has not revealed this to you, but my Father who is in heaven. And I tell you, you are Peter, and on this rock I will build my Church, and the gates of hell shall not prevail against it." Matthew 16:16–18

Some Christian denominations, such as the Catholic Church, interpret this verse to mean that Peter is the rock upon which the Church was founded, and for that reason, Peter is considered to be the first Pope. However, Protestants, as well as other denominations, interpret this verse differently. Though many believe that Jesus' reference here to Peter's name as the "*rock*," was no sovereignty given to him by Christ, rather, Jesus was referring to Peter's declaration: *"You are the Christ, the Son of the living God."* This confession of faith is the rock upon which the Church is built, and just like Peter, everyone who confesses Jesus Christ as Lord is a part of the Church.

The Ekklesia (a political term) - the assembly, the called, those who are call out. The ecclesia or ekklesia (ἐκκλησία) was the principal assembly of the democracy of ancient Athens during its "Golden Ages.

(Christianity or Ecclesiastical) in formal church usage is the congregation.

(Historically) it was the assembly of citizens of an ancient Greek state from Medieval Latin and Late Greek.

It was the popular assembly, opened only to all male citizens with two years of military service: meaning that all classes of citizens in Athens were not able to participate in government; historically there was the "*thetes*" a form of government where only property owners were allowed to participate; a second definition state that it is a form of government where love and honor are the ruling principles. The ekklesia opened the doors for all citizens, regardless of class, to nominate and vote for magistrates; likewise, the church of today is open to all who will submit to the teaching of Jesus Christ, and like the second definition, love and honor (respect) are the ruling principles as found in the fruit of the spirit.

The local church is defined as a local assembly of believers or a congregation that meets together physically for worship, fellowship, teaching, prayer, and encouragement in the faith. Paul warns us to not to forget to come together.

> *Not forsaking the assembling of ourselves together, as the manner of some is; but exhorting one another: and so much the more, as ye see the day approaching*
>
> *(Hebrews 10:25). KJV)*

At the local church level, we are able to live in relationship with other believers—we break bread together *(Communion),* pray for each other, and disciple and strengthen one another. At the same time, all believers are members of the Universal Church. The Universal Church is made up of every single person who has exercised faith in Jesus Christ for salvation, including members of every local church body throughout the earth.

> *For by one Spirit are we all baptized into one body, whether we be Jews or Gentiles, whether we be bond or free; and have been all made to drink into one Spirit.*
>
> *(1 Corinthians 12:13; Ephesians 1:22-23).*

So, who is the church?

The founder of the "home church" movement in England, Canon Ernest Southcott, said it best:

> *"The holiest moment of the <u>church service</u> is the moment when God's people—strengthened by preaching and sacrament—go out of the church door into the world to be the church. We don't go to church; we are the church."*

The church, therefore, is not a place. It's not the building, it's not the location, and it's not the denomination. We, God's people who are in Christ Jesus, are the church.

The purpose of the church

The purpose of the church is two-fold. First and foremost, the church comes together (assembles) for the purpose of bringing each member to spiritual maturity.

> *Till we all come in the unity of the faith, and of the knowledge of the Son of God, unto a perfect man, unto the measure of the stature of the fullness of Christ:*
>
> *(Ephesians 4:13). KJV*

Secondly, the church reaches out (to the scattered) to spread the love of Christ and His gospel message to unbelievers in the world.

> *And Jesus came and spake unto them, saying, All power is given unto me in heaven and in earth. Go ye therefore, and teach all nations, baptizing them in the name of the Father, and of the Son, and of the Holy Ghost: Teaching them to observe all things whatsoever I have commanded you: and, lo, I am with you always, even unto the end of the world.*
>
> *(Matthew 28:18-20) KJV*

This is the Great Commission. So, the purpose of the church is to minister to both, believers and unbelievers. The church, in both, the universal and local sense, is important because it is one of the main vehicles through which God carries out his purposes on earth. The church is the body of Christ — His heart, His mouth, His hands and His feet, reaching out to the world.

> *Now ye are the body of Christ and every member an individual part of it.*
>
> *(1 Corinthians 12:27)*

THE BIRTH OF A CHURCH

Just as new parents prepare for the arrival of a new child into their family, a visionary must prepare for the birthing of a new church or ministry. God creates the circumstances, pull together the resources and choses individuals necessary for the healthy birthing of a new ministry. But the Church, the mystical body of Christ, was born at Calvary by the redemptive death of Jesus Christ; it was on the Day of Pentecost when the Holy Spirit introduced the Church to the world so that the whole of humanity (all who submit to the teaching of Jesus Christ) would be transformed into a "Peculiar People" as was Israel, the Old Testament Church, was formed in the wilderness. Thus God made a new Covenant with the Church connected to Christ by his redemptive blood.

> *In the same manner He also took the cup after supper, saying, "This cup is the new covenant in My blood. This do, as often as you drink it, in remembrance of Me." For as often as you eat this bread and drink this cup, you proclaim the Lord's death till He comes.*
>
> *1 Corinthians 11:25-26*

Out of the Church came churches, ministries and other unctions of the Holy Spirit according to God's predestined will for every believer who became a disciple of Christ; it is the birth of these ministries about which I wish to focus. Birthing is a process which occurs over a period of time and after several stages of preparation.

Every believer is mandated by the Word of God to be a witness of the Gospel of Jesus Christ, but every believer has not been chosen to give birth to ministry as a church leader or visionary.

Purpose come from God; "Except the LORD build the house, they labour in vain that build it." To be set apart for the Master's work one must be proven worthy. All women appear physically capable of giving birth, but all are not able to.

> *"And he gave some, apostles; and some, prophets; and some, evangelists; and some, pastors and teachers; For the perfecting of the saints, for the work of the ministry, for the edifying of the body of Christ:*
>
> *Ephesians 4:11-12*

Many believers may have the potential of giving birth to ministry, but access will only be endowed to those who endured a process that proves their readiness; "few are chosen." Ambition and academia are not enough to mandate a call to ministerial leadership; ambition motivates while at the same time mandates an increased focus on a specific interest; focus enhances one's knowledge of his or her ministerial ability; it is the measure of a leader's desire to turn his or her commitment into reality. As important as ambition is in achieving one's visionary purpose, it can create a problem when it is contaminated with over zealousness or has too much ambitious potential; there is a saying, "Those who are not humble will stumble on their way to greatness" and "a driving ambition is of little use if you are on the wrong road" (Pearl Bailey).

The birth of any ministry must first occur in the mind of God; God knew our ways, ordered our footsteps, and predestined our purpose before we were born; our course had been charted and our call to ministry approved.

God spoke to Jeremiah and said "before you were conceived, before you were formed in your mother's belly, I knew you; not only did I know you, I place my stamp of approval on your life and predestined your purpose; I called you to be a prophet, not locally but nationally to the nations. The Lord said, "For I know the thoughts that I think toward you, thoughts of peace, and not of evil, to bring you to an expected end. Because your call as a visionary is the predestined will of God and has been manifested to you through prophetic revelation does not mean that the birthing of your ministry will be without challenge and opposition.

Paul knew his calling and was committed to turning his vision into reality; amidst persecution he was charged to give birth to a new church in Thessalonica; the church met with severe challenge right from the start; notwithstanding other difficulties; the church was overly inundated with unbelievers who voiced to its member that Paul was not a true Apostle of God. Paul was forced to remind the church of Thessalonica of the trouble he and those with him had in Philippi and how outrageously he and those who were with him were treated for Christ's sake (I Thessalonians 2). Paul then defends his ministry against those accusations. He wrote in verses 3 and 4 (niv)

> *You know brothers and sisters that our visit to you was not without results. [2] We had previously suffered and been treated outrageously in Philippi, as you know, but with the help of our God we dared to tell you his gospel in the face of strong opposition.*
>
> *Thessalonians 2:1-2*

No matter how carefully you plan the birth of your ministry, you will meet opposition to its validity; either by challenging the necessity of its existence or your worthiness as its visionary; the birthing stage of ministry is Satan's last chance to stop it from turning your vision into reality; he will test the commitment you have toward your calling as a visionary, and challenge your faith in God to be more than a conquer in bring you to your expected end. As a visionary you have but one obligation that is to obey God; if God tells you to jump through a wall, your obligation is to jump; it is God's job to move the wall; face your challenges and stand on God's promises.

> *For the appeal we make does not spring from error or impure motives, nor are we trying to trick you. [4] On the contrary, we speak as those approved by God to be entrusted with the*

> *gospel. We are not trying to please people but God, who tests our hearts.*[5]
>
> *I Thessalonians 2:3-4 NIV*

Here the word "approved" means that God had tested their worthiness and that they have passed the test. Paul is saying that "God has set His seal of approval on my ministry." As we look closely at this passage, we find that there are characteristics of Paul's ministry that needs to be a part of every believer's ministry if he or she is to please God as a visionary leader.

> *You know we never used flattery, nor did we put on a mask to cover up greed—God is our witness. We were not looking for praise from people, not from you or anyone else, even though as apostles of Christ we could have asserted our authority.*[7] *Instead, we were like young children*[a] *among you*
>
> *I Thessalonians 2:5-7 NIV.*

Birthing a ministry approved by God requires commitment to the oracles of God, the principle of the doctrine, and to true Holiness. Lukewarm and halfhearted commitment will never lead to the establishment of a church or an organized body of believer that will serve God in true of Holiness. "Upon this rock I build my church," Peter had just referred to Jesus as "The Christ," Jesus' response was, you have called me a name expressive of my character, therefore Peter, likewise will I change your name to fit your character, "Thou art Peter, a rock," denoting firmness, solidity, and stability; and "upon this rock I will build my Church." The visionary of any ministry must be firm, especially the leaders of a newly developing ministries; however large or small, the foundation of any ministry must be sure.

I've lived in New York City all my life where there is not a day that goes by when one does not encounter some kind of construction; it always begins with the gathering of all kinds of special equipment for the job. Barriers are erected to protect the public from the dangers associated with the process of building; during the process the public is force to detour or to walk on temporary sidewalks and under plywood canapés; sometimes the workers can be heard doing their job down in a large hold; sometime it takes months or even years to see evidence of the building, depending on the size of the structure being erected; then as if out of nowhere, the building's skeletal structure appears, revealing the soon-to-come enormous building that would occupy a once empty space. No matter how impressive the building would one day be, its structural integrity is dependent upon the firmness of its foundation.

When birthing a new ministry, it is necessary to build it on a firm foundation; its leaders must have spiritual integrity; like the construction of the sky scraper, the viability of the structure depends on the soundness of the foundation's base. The importance of having a sure foundation is a lesson for all believers, especially for visionary leaders when it comes to their spiritual lives. The integrity of a building is predicated upon the types of materials used in its construction. In the same way every believer and every spiritual leader must be mindful of his or her spiritual works and the principles on which they are built. It is not enough to be a hearer; one must be a doer of God's commandments; those who hear and do are like a wise man who builds on a foundation that is set upon a rock.

> *Therefore, everyone who hears these words of mine and puts them into practice is like a wise man who built his house on the rock. The rain came down, the streams rose, and the winds blew and beat against that house; yet it did not fall, because it had its foundation on the rock*
>
> *Matthew 7:24 and 25*

One of the foundational pillars of every successful ministry is integrity; people only follow leaders who they can trust; losing the trust of people is a recipe for failure. Paul boasted of the trust that church leaders developed for his ministry and said:

> *"Our conscience testifies that we have conducted ourselves in the world, especially in our relations with you, in the holiness and sincerity that are from God."*
>
> *2 Corinthians 1:12*

Paul is saying….no one can say that we have done anything to be ashamed of when it comes to the preaching and teaching of God's Word; we have done it with integrity and with a clear conscious. Titus tells us that leaders must be above reproach, speaking sound doctrine, showing integrity and reverence so that no one can say anything evil about them. Integrity includes morality, greed, and credibility. If you say something, do it.

THE SERVANT'S HEART

To give birth to a healthy ministry one must have a servant's heart; a heart that has been circumcised; I know when you hear the word "circumcise" you think of the physical, but circumcision is a type of covenant God attached to His promises made to Abraham.

> *This is my covenant, which you shall keep, between me and you and your descendants after you: every male among you shall be circumcised. And you shall be circumcised in the flesh of your foreskin; and it shall be the sign of the covenant between Me and you. And every male among you who is eight days old shall be circumcised throughout your generations, a servant who is born in the house or who is bought with money from any foreigner, who is not of your descendants. A servant who is born in your house or who is bought with your money shall surely be circumcised; thus shall My covenant be in your flesh for an everlasting covenant."*
>
> Genesis 17:10-13

The key phrase here is "sign" or "token of the covenant between you and Me;" if we continue to read Leviticus 12:3 we find that it becomes a part of the Law of Moses. The practice of circumcision sat Israel apart from other nations and made them God's chosen people. As believers we, the Church, must have circumcised heart, and cut away anything that might hinder the work of God in our lives.

> *"Moreover, the Lord your God will circumcise your heart and the heart of your descendants, to love the Lord your God with all your heart and with all your soul, in order that you may live."*
>
> Deuteronomy 30:6

Circumcise then your heart, and stiffen your neck no more

Deuteronomy 10:16

"For thus says the Lord to the men of Judah and to Jerusalem, "Break up your fallow ground, and do not sow among thorns. Circumcise yourselves to the Lord and remove the foreskins of your heart, Men of Judah and inhabitants of Jerusalem, or else My wrath will go forth like fire and burn with none to quench it, because of the evil of your deeds."

Jeremiah 4:3-4

"And in Him you were also circumcised with a circumcision made without hands, in the removal of the body of the flesh by the circumcision of Christ; having been buried with Him in baptism, in which you were also raised up with Him through faith in the working of God, who raised Him from the dead. When you were dead in your transgressions and the uncircumcision of your flesh, He made you alive together with Him, having forgiven us all our transgressions,"

Colossians 2:11-13

THE THEOCRACY OF THE CHURCH

Too often does the politics of ministry interfere with visionary purpose; this is not to say that there should not be a system that demonstrates agreement and unity among leaders and visionaries, but there are times when what seems right and fool proof to the majority, may not be the predestined will of God. The Church is a theocracy and not a democracy, nor is it an autocracy; the leadership of the Church comes from God and not the voice of the majority. Because the Church is a theocracy, the Word of God becomes its authority and takes president over any decision that is made regarding its operation. In a season where individual church goers pride themselves on what church they attend, it should be noted that the Church does not belong to any denomination. This mystical body of believers belongs to Jesus Christ. The leadership and oversight of church functions was given to the Elders in Acts 20:28.

> *And I say also unto thee, that thou art Peter, and upon this rock I will build my church; and the gates of hell shall not prevail against it.*
>
> Matthew 16:18

> "*Take heed therefore unto yourselves, and to all the flock, over the which the Holy Ghost hath made you overseers, to feed the church of God, which He hath purchased with his own blood.*"
>
> Act 20:28

Paul wrote to the Elders in the Church of Ephesus saying, "Feed the flock;" the Elders cannot feed the flock unless they know its needs; the Elders at their consecration were admonished to guard the faith, and to study to show themselves approved so that they can feed the flock of God, but most of all, be living epistles (examples) so that they can also lead the flock. When church members and subordinate ministers start to feel that the visionary (pastor), who by the inspiration of God, gave birth to the ministry, have to answer to them as to what kind of job he or she is doing as visionaries, the ministry is on the road to failure. The people should have input and give feedback, but their opinions are not the most import factor when it comes to making decisions that affect God's Divine purpose for the church. Paul wrote to the church at Corinth concerning judgement of his works. As visionaries we all must stand before the owner of the sheepfold and give account of our leadership as Shepherd of God's flock.

> *"But with me it is a very small thing that I should be judged of you, or of man's judgment: yea, I judge not mine own self. For I know nothing by myself; yet am I not hereby justified: but he that judgeth me is the Lord.*
>
> 1 Corinthians 4:3-4

The final authority as to who governs and how to govern one's commitment and dedication to visionary purpose is the Word of God. God has revealed His methods to some degree in every book of the Bible: historical, prophetic, poetic, and in the epistle. In them there is a depiction of the heart and mind of God's Will for His people, and every leader of the Church must come to know it and feel the pulse of God in his or her relationship with the it, and for the works God has purposed for it. All believers are not serving God at the same level of Holiness; therefore, there are different levers of anointing and discernment in Church fellowship. As the leader of a newly formed ministry it is imperative that you know the spiritual maturity of those to whom you commit subordinate leadership. Leaders without servant hearts can easily influence an atmosphere of carnality among followers. Carnality leads to the challenge of authority, focus on the democratic process, and the right to question unpopular decisions.

No Church will ever be free of challenge, even if it has but one member and that member is the visionary. Paul found that even in himself there were challenges; the things he would do, he said "I do not, and the things I would not do, I do." What is important in birthing a ministry is not the challenges of the ministry; it is the process by which these challenges are resolved. Challenge is the mother of resolution; it forces one to develop vision that meets the challenges while at the same time see him or herself out of the situation that created the challenge.

Another major challenge to newly formed ministries is administrative (recordkeeping); keeping in touch with the members of the fellowship; following up on issues that concern ministry is as important as evangelism itself. It is not uncommon for an individual to join a church on his or her first visit and never return; a good recordkeeping and follow-up program will win some of these one-visit believers while at the same time enhance the growth and development of the ministry. Newly formed ministries will face challenge in almost every aspect of ministry, but in the process of meeting those challenges, the leaders of the ministry will learn to feel the pulse of the ministry. There are currents that run through ministries; these currents can adversely affect the growth and development of its members and derail its progress toward visionary reality; currents are like the wind; they may be as gentle as a summer breeze are as devastating as a winter storm; their origin varies from, "that's not the way the former pastor use to do it" to "I've been in the church from the start and I…" Every challenge has the potential to become a contrary wind that is design to delay God purpose for visionary reality. Every pastor, especially new leaders, must constantly monitor the atmosphere within the ministry and feel the pulse of the people of God over which oversight has been given. Challenge is not only a basis for vision, it also strengthens the leader's resolve to endure hardness as a good soldier.

God never intended to give His Divine Power and Authority over into the hands of man so that he might do as he please. Every visionary purpose in both heaven and earth must be in accordance to the predestined will of our Almighty God. God never meant for man to feel that he had a free hand in regard to commitment without accountability on earth, as well as in heaven, for his actions.

Theocratic leadership has been in effect from the dawn of time. God's divine plan of sovereign leadership or ruler over man's actions regarding the pastoring of the people and the Church was established in the garden when God assigned Adam to supervise His creation. Notice that the authority of God took president as He gave Adam directions as to how to attend the garden. The responsibility and terms of Adam's rule over the thing in the garden were positive and unmistakable.

> *And God blessed them, and God said unto them, be fruitful, and multiply, and replenish the earth, and subdue it: and have dominion over the fish of the sea, and over the fowl of the air, and over every living thing that moveth upon the earth. And God said, Behold, I have given you every herb bearing seed, which is upon the face of all the earth, and every tree, in the which is the fruit of a tree yielding seed; to you it shall be for meat. And to every beast of the earth, and to every fowl of the air, and to everything that creepeth upon the earth, wherein there is life, I have given every green herb for meat: and it was so.*
>
> *Genesis 1:28-30*

In like manner there are limitations as to man's authority and lordship over the Church; man's will and power under God was clearly stated.

> *And the LORD God commanded the man, saying, of every tree of the garden thou mayest freely eat:*
>
> *But of the tree of the knowledge of good and evil, thou shalt not eat of it: for in the day that thou eatest thereof thou shalt surely die.*
>
> *Genesis 2:16-17*

This was pure Theocratic leadership – man supervising God's creation in direct harmony and obedience to His Word. Man was not free to do as he thought, he only experienced peace and sweet fellowship as long as he followed and obeyed the laws God had established. This was the very beginning of man's relationship with God, and it was based on obedience. Then suddenly, man fail to live up to his part through willful disobedience, thus introducing sin into his relationship with God. Adam, created in God's image, became a carnal man with a rebellious nature. This nature is a part of every man born on the face of the earth. No longer is a man born in innocence. No longer is man born in God's likeness and in His image. The Bible states:

> *And Adam lived an hundred and thirty years, and begat a son in his own likeness, and after his image; and called his name Seth:*
>
> *Genesis 5:3*

Because of carnal rebelliousness man would here after produce kind after his kind, generation after generation of sinful children in rebellion against God's divine order and authority. No carnal man wants to be told what to do. Yet God has divinely willed men to obey His law administered by His ordained administrators (Pastor, Elder, etc.).

LOVE AND DISCIPLESHIP

You may ask where does love fit into the making of church; love is the essential element of developing a ministry; without it, it is impossible to develop a relationship with God or his people; you may be able to start a ministry, but it won't be a part of the Church; it may be a church or an organization but not the Church. Love is what it does; let us look at love from the perspective of "Eros" the love that transcend us to immobility, that connects us to God. Most people experience the form of love known as philia, love that attracts body to body, human to human, personal; it may be utilitarian, that which is useful like a washing machine; it could be romantic which leads to marriage; it could be humanitarian where one prescribes to the idea that they love everybody in general, but really doesn't love anybody in particular. In reality, philia love is born out of Eros and in return need Eros to strengthen itself.

Love is the first fruit of the spirit; it is what all human emotion is built upon; without love no relationship can flourish; love is the foundation of the church, without it we cannot please God; it is like faith; love connects us to God; "for God so loved the world that He gave His only begotten son." self-love is a prerequisite to loving others. If one does not love him or her-self how than can he or she love anyone else. If a fat man hates himself because he is fat, then he possibly will hate all fat men.

One must not only love church, but he must love what he does in the church, the work of the ministry. serving others; Going to church is one of the instructions God gave the believers; "not forsaking the assembling of ourselves together" Hebrew 10:25. We go to church to worship, but the greatest moment of the believer is when he leaves the church to become the Church. In reality each member of the congregation is the church; we must be "living epistle." We may be the only church some unbeliever every see.

Man must love God with all his heart, soul, and might, then love his neighbor as he loves himself. Only then is one able to receive everything good from God and to serve one's neighbors with everything one has. The self-giving divine (agape) love gives to each of us our existence, goodness, beauty, righteousness, strength, wisdom, and wealth. In this sense, everything comes from God.

Discipleship

In the development of a new ministry one of the basic concerns of the visionary must be discipleship; everyone connected to the vision must understand his or her role as a disciple. The term "disciple" means "learner, pupil, follower, or apprentice;" it means "thought accompanied by endeavor;" to become a disciple means to follow someone, to learn from that person. To become a disciple is to imitate the way one's master does a thing and the process in which he or she pursuit to turn vision into reality. The Bible uses the term disciple in different ways:

Following the leader - becoming a disciple does not make one a righteous man, nor does it make one a serious believer. Many followed Jesus; some for bread, some for the miracles, some for the blessings, and other for the sake of saying, " I was there." The leaders of the Church, the visionaries must create a picture in the minds of the congregation that clearly outlines the reality of their purpose and how to transform each of their lives to be instruments of God, turning vision into reality by following them as they follow Christ.

Jesus challenged His follows to consider the cost of being a "true" disciple; the same must be true in ministry today. There is a physical as well as spiritual sacrifice attached to discipleship and to becoming a fellow laborer in the Lord's Church. Time, gifts, obedience, commitment, dedication, and devotion are as important to ministry as sacrifice. Jesus identified three principles of becoming His disciple: A person must love Him above all other relationship (Luke 14:26), be steadfast, even threw suffering or death, to commit all to Him. Discipleship means committing one's whole life to Christ, both spiritual and secular gifts. You will know who is on your team by what they do and by how they submit to your teaching. Jesus said to the Jews who were with him, "if you hold to my teaching, you are my disciples." (John 8:32.) The translation of "hold" means "to abide" or "continue." There is a mark difference between being a hearer and being a doer; one cannot just listen and be considered a disciple; this relationship calls for obedience which is the heart of discipleship. Dedication, devotion, and obedience must be the standard for the Church.

As the Church grew and spread throughout Greece; after the persecution of the early Church leaders and the stoning of Stephen, the disciples scattered throughout the Mediterranean world. As the Church grew in the Greek city of Antioch, Barnabas, who was sent to Jerusalem to minister to a new set of believers, sent for Paul to come help him teach the rapidly growing Gentile Church; it was in Antioch where the disciples were first called Christians. The term disciple now changed to Christian was perhaps the most notable change in the New Testament Church. There are different viewpoints as to why the change was necessary; one is that the new Gentile Christian wanted an identity that was not associated with the distinctive Jewish culture; others say that the term "Christian" would eliminate what was a too ambiguous association with the more general term disciple; but because the Church had become more Gentile/Greek in its identity, the theory is that the change was associated with the etymology of the word; this is understandable. Thus, the term Christian was seen as more descriptive of who they were following. Within the Roman society "ian" added to the end of a proper name signified total allegiance to that person. Thus, Christian became a very clear term connecting absolute loyalty to Christ.

The term Christian early in the Gentile Church carried the same distinctive meaning as disciple; therefor many Christians died for their faith at the hands of Roman authority. Persecution and suffering only served to make Christians stronger.

WHY THE CHURCH MUST BE ORGANIZED

As foretasted the word "Church" is translated from the Greek "ecclesia" meaning "called out." The Church is God's called-out, blood-washed believers who are reserved unto Him for a Bride. Jesus gave His life for the Church; the Church has been chosen as the source through which salvation is attained; those who submit to the calling, surrenders to the highest calling of the ages; because of this the Church must be an institution of order.

Paul in his letter to the church at Ephesus said, "we, the church, must be without spot or wrinkle." Peter added, "and without blemish." The Church cannot accomplish this Godly character and maturity without order and discipline. Biblical, order does not mean the crystallization of worship or sugarcoating the oracles of God, nor does it bring a clamping down on the demonstration of the Holy Spirit. It does mean that we should exercise true Holiness unto the Lord with righteousness and obedience to the Word of God. The Epistles warns us of the necessity for order in the church.

Paul (Titus 1:3-5), admonished Titus according to the commandments of God, to "set in order the things that are wanting in the Church of Crete." He writes to the Church at Corinth, according to the commandments of God "Let all things be done decently and in order;" he teaches them that "God is not the author of confusion." To assure that the Church is in order, Peter in the 4th chapter tells us that "judgement will start at the house of God." Another pattern of order is demonstrated in the 19th chapter of Mark where Jesus feeds the multitude of 5000. Notice the order in which the miracle is performed: He first divides the multitude in companies of hundreds and fifties, He blessed and broke the bread, gave it to the disciples, and instructed them to give it to the people.

The pattern in which ministers and elders (pastors) is to server the Church is an orderly one. God gives the Word and the leaders in ministry gives it to the people or congregation. God gave the responsibility of restoring man to an acceptable state of Grace to Church leadership; He is a God of order. When Paul asked the Lord, "what must I do to be saved," Jesus could have told him, but the pattern had been set, the responsibility had been given to man, the preacher; therefore, Jesus said to Paul, "go to Damascus, there you will meet a man named Ananias, he will tell you what to do." Likewise, when Lazarus was in the bosoms of Abraham, the rich man asked that he be allowed to go back to earth and warn his brother not to come to hell, the Lord said that responsibility belongs to the elders and the prophets. God is a God of order.

When Jesus sent out the seventy, He told them how to go (two by two) how to pray, what to say; not to go from house to house (only where I lead you); what they should eat, what works they were to preform, and what to do if they were rejected.

As leaders of the people of God we are to work toward developing mature leaders and followers of God who will submit to an orderly form of Church administration. Carnal man watches every move that the Church makes and takes advantage of every flaw it perceives that Church makes. Many in the carnal world do not want to see the Church organized and orderly. Sadly, I must say there are some within ministry who fight the theocratic form of Church leadership that God Himself has established to assure that He, and He alone is the source of every inspiration that Church leadership gets. That is why the Church is a theocracy.

LEADERSHIP THAT HINDERS THE MOVE OF GOD

The most prominent form of Church leadership today is democratic church leadership; and perhaps a form of it is in almost every church, including the holiest of ministries. When the Lord returns to receive His bride, it is this form of church leadership that will cause many to be rejected as part of the Lord's bride. Churches that have elected boards that limits the visionary purpose of its leaders by demanding that church program and the reality of pastoral vision be determined by a vote to decide whether they can fulfill an unction of the Holy Spirit are out of order. Vision inspired by the Holy Spirit must not be held hostage by church leaders who operates from a democratic perspective.

The democratic form of leadership is what Jesus will find when He returns; John has already seen it in Revelations 3:14-19, a church governed and moved by the attitude and will of the people, the will of the majority, the Laodicean church; the leadership was not move by the Will of God, but by worldly lust and materialism. I'm comfortable with saying that if there were leaders in the Leodicean church who would have had the unction to do the will of God, they would have been outnumbered and outcast.

> *For the time will come when they will not endure sound doctrine; but after their own lusts shall they heap to themselves teachers, having itching ears; And they shall turn away their ears from the truth, and shall be turned unto fables.*
>
> *II Timothy 4:3-4*

When the voice of the people overrules the guidance of the Holy Spirit, the leadership of the Church is in error. But the question remains, just how much authority does the pastor have? Let's look at Moses, God's pastor in the wilderness; there will always be those who oppose the direction in which God is leading the Church because of their carnality and lack of commitment. Some feel that because they too are saved that they can also hear from God in regards to ministry and leadership. Two separate incidents occurred during Moses' leadership that will help us understand the power God has vested in His chosen leaders.

> *And they gathered themselves together against Moses and against Aaron, and said unto them, Ye take too much upon you, seeing all the congregation are holy, every one of them, and the LORD is among them: wherefore then lift ye up yourselves above the congregation of the LORD?*
>
> Numbers 16:3

Verses 28-33 gives the result of this rebellion against Moses' leadership; the earth opens at Moses' command and Korah and his company were swallowed up. This emphatically demonstrates that God does back up his chosen leaders. Numbers 12th chapter gives another example of God's support of His leaders.

> *And they said, Hath the LORD indeed spoken only by Moses? hath he not spoken also by us? And the LORD heard it*
>
> Numbers 12:2

The story continues with the subsequence judgment of leprosy falling upon Miriam; this leprosy represented God's disapproval of Miriam and Aaron's rebellion against God's chosen leadership; it also represented a type of sin which brings us to the words that David clearly rings in our ears:

> *Touch not mine anointed, and do my prophets no harm.*
>
> Psalm 105:15

In many ways democratic leadership weakens the role of the pastor; it in some ways limits his ability to administer according to the leading of the Holy Spirit. In some cases, when dealing with church discipline and setting the standards of Holiness, which involving certain members of the board of administrators, pastors have been voted out; in other instance, the pastor is a hireling; he comes and goes at the people's bidding; in such cases the people have no shepherd over them. Jesus gave an example of the good shepherds in opposed to the hireling.

> *I am the good shepherd: the good shepherd giveth his life for the sheep. But he that is an hireling, and not the shepherd, whose own the sheep are not, seeth the wolf coming, and leaveth the sheep, and fleeth: and the wolf catcheth them, and scattereth the sheep. The hireling fleeth, because he is an hireling, and careth not for the sheep.*
>
> *John 10:11-13*

When the democratic process take president over the leading of God's spirits, the political processes promotes individuals in leadership who put their favorite candidate in position; carnal spirits emerge and dissention along with displeasure among believes immerges. Many times those who were voted out retain hard feeling toward those who were vote in to replace them; under Theocratic leadership promotion come by the divine inspiration of God and not by the inclination of man.

VISION

Let me close by making some comment on vision; vision is the most important prenatal development in preparation for the birthing of a church; the visionary must know precisely what God has shown him or her and where he or she is going. "If you don't know where you are going, you will end up somewhere else." If the visionary does not have a clear picture of what God had shown him or her the enemy will do all it can to further distort or destroy the vision. The job of the visionary is to hold to what God has given. Vision is not limited to the birthing of a church; it is attached to every purpose given to men; along with vision comes time and destiny. We have no inclination of time; it is in the hands of God; our responsibility is to step into purpose before we exhaust time. The enemy of vision is fear; to achieve purpose we must overcome fear. Fear is designed to keep us where we are: without faith, broken and living in poverty, uneducated and without spiritual development. God has not given us a spirit of fear, but of power and love and a sound mind. When we speak of fear we do not speak of servile fear (enslaving); we speak of filial fear (fear that relate to son-ship), The Hebrew word for fear is "yare" means to fear, to respect, to reverence.

Fear is the foundation for instruction and knowledge; for the fear of God is the beginning of wisdom. Fear keeps the visionary focused on what God has promised while at the same time, enduring the challenges of opposition. The enemy use temporal fear to distract, distort, and dissuade us from obeying God; he paints a picture of an unattainable pursuit of purpose. As visionaries we must focus on past experiences of God's blessing toward us to fortify our trust in Him.

When we consider the essential traits of a visionary, we might list prayer, logic, reason, intellect as the first principles. While these are necessary parts of becoming a visionary they do not offer a complete description of a visionary as understood by me as a church leader. The visionary's life does not just entail thinking or studying but consists of a whole pattern of commitment, dedication and devotion. As such, becoming a visionary is not an academic discipline but a spiritual exercise encompassing the whole of life. Nothing spiritually should be neglected when it comes to one's commitment as the visionary seeking to order his or her life. This entails developing parts of life like virtue, integrity, the practice of severe self-discipline, control of the passions, and detachment from worldly and bodily concerns, such as lust. Being a visionary also requires prayer. Prayer is not a secondary concern in the life of a visionary's, it is an essential component of desiring wisdom. To understand this one must understand that to lead a visionary's life is to ascent or journey in the divine presence of God. The visionary who desires wisdom, who seeks to be wise and virtuous, which means to become lead by the spirit is not something that a person can achieve on his or her own. Becoming a visionary is not done in isolation; the visionary depends on having the right kind of company. In the scripture we have "the school of the Prophets" visionaries must keep company with God, men should always pray.

We must consider the relationship of prayer and the word we choose and how they support our petition. Prayer is a necessary component of the visionary's life as it keeps him or her in company with God through interceding for others and through personal petition. Not only is the visionary admonished to stay in the presence of God, but every believer is to pray without ceasing.

PART TWO

THE UNDERROWER

We have a little sister, and she hath no breasts: what shall we do for our sister in the day when she shall be spoken for?

Song of Solomon 8:8 KJV

Solomon here is dealing with two metaphors, both representing a church; one, the Jewish Church and the other, the New Testament Church which includes the engrafted Gentile Church. One is described as His wife and the other His "Little Sister." He expresses His love for her (the Jewish Church) and she for Him. He discusses with His espoused wife His concern for their little sister (the Gentile Church); I would go as far as to say, His concern for the Church in general. She is richly endowed, her body developed, pleasing to look upon, able to attract the attention of the opposite sex; perhaps capable of satisfying her intended in bed, but she has no breast. If she conceives and give birth; she has no breast; she cannot provide the nourishment that sustains life. They (in their pious state) saw the condition of their sister as deplorable, pitiful.

They, the two churches, are sisters, children of the same fathers, God and Adam, but the little sisters, the Gentile Churches are not dignified with the knowledge of God's manifestations; they have no breasts, no divine revelation, no scriptures, no ministers, no breasts with sustaining consolation drawn out to them; when they might suck, being strangers to the covenants of promise, they have no milk to sustain their children, to nourish them. Peter, preaching to the Jeddah Christians in 1 Peter 2:2

(*Like newborn babies, crave pure spiritual milk, so that by it you may grow up in your salvation, now that you have tasted that the Lord is good.* NIV)

The Church today is not the same Church I grew up in where the members showed respect to leadership, express a desire to learn more of God and how to please Him. A place where the love of God took president over the life of its members and where growing into maturity as a Christian was first and foremost. A church where, we as member, could not ware anything we wanted to church, but had to dress modestly. We have a little sister; she has no breast; What shall we do for her?

> *Let a man so account of us, as of the ministers of Christ, and stewards of the mysteries of God.*
>
> *1 Corinthians 4:1*

Paul here writes to the church at Corinth, not being please with their perception of him and the other apostles as ministers, tried to dissuade them with temperate words to look at them as servant and stewards of God. It is important to listen to the tone of Paul's letter. Often we are in the right when trying to explain our position, but in doing so we use emotionally loaded words. We must remember that *the power of death and life is in the tongue: and they that love it shall eat the fruit thereof. Proverbs 18:21.*

There may be times when we will, as Paul was, be faced with disrespect because others disagree with our elevations in ministry; while elevation may place us at a different level of leadership, it is not a license to become arrogant or superfluous; it should add to our character humility and humbleness. Paul said to the church at Corinth, regardless of our accomplishments and our levels of anointing or our disposition; we are ministers and servants of the Most High. By putting himself in the category of minister and not referring to himself as the chief apostle, he humbly submits to the office of a servant (the Greek word "huperetes" or Underrower); then he, without showing them up, shows them the proper way to treat or care for those who labor in the Gospel as ministers. Solomon said, "What shall we do for her? She has no breast."

This book is about those who bear the responsibility of turning the believer's commitment into visionary reality. Where there is no vision, the people perish. Vision is the driving force that pushes us toward our divine purpose. The visionary charts the course, and through divine guidance, leads the fellowship to the place God has purposed it to be.

When we think of the underrower we think of the ancient mariners that use slaves to row their big ships across the sea; the structure of the ship was such that there was a galley and a sub-galley; it was in the sub-galley where slaves who rowed the ship were bounded to their task; they abode there throughout the entire voyage; their only job was to row; the direction of the ship was not their concern; the purpose of the journey was not their concern, neither was the route the shipmaster chose.

The Greek word for minister is "huperetes", an underrower (hupo, [under], eretes, [rower]). The slaves who were the rowers called the task of rowing "awako" (Awako- Yoruba)

> *As underrowers for the cause of Christ, we are not slaves but debtor of Christ for "He was wounded for our transgressions and bruised for our iniquities, the transgression of our peace was upon Him, and by his scripts we are healed."*
>
> Isaiah 53:5

Slave or servant, from what perspective do you see your labor as a member of the body of Christ? In the Church, it is not rowing that makes the slave a servant; it is his willingness to be submissive while rowing according to directions. A rower's circumstance may make him a slave but his disposition under those circumstances will determine the level of his stewardship.

The servant (member of the church) doesn't dictate his own course, but willingly and submissively yield to the authority and directions of another for the sake of accomplishing visionary purpose; as rowers, in a secular setting, worked together at the command of a supervisor to move a mighty ship through the water; as believers we must work together to accomplish that which is the predestined will of God; this is done through obedience to visionary leaders whom the Lord has place over the Church. We are many members, making up the Body of Christ and supporters of visionary purpose. The visionary is also a servant who has been given oversight over the members of the congregation and must "*declare to them the whole counsel of God,*" *Acts 20:26-27*

The secret to fulfillment as an underrower in the church is the ability to work with others in ministry; even in a one-man row boat there has to be coordination and continuity, otherwise the boat will simply go around in circles; individually, the right hand and the left hand must push and pull together. As a member of a ministry, you must work with others members of the church to turn the vision of the visionary into reality; underrowing requires teamwork, endurance, perseverance, and of course, commitment, dedication, and devotion without such, vision cannot become reality.

One does not wake up one morning and expect to be placed on his local church ministerial team just because he has decided to become a minister; stewardship requires preparation, first and foremost, faithfulness. The unfaithful steward hinders the progress of ministry; understanding doctrine or vision may not be a prerequisite for the call to ministry, but faithfulness is. Saul of Tosha was faithful to what he believed to be the will of God; although he misinterpreted God's plan of salvation and caused havoc in the Church, he was called to be an apostle because of his faithfulness. Being faithful, prayerful, devoted and studious are important characteristics in preparation for stewardship; but we must *study to show thou self approval, as workman not to be ashamed right dividing the word of truth.*

2 Timothy 2:15.

TURE SERVANTS OF CHRIST

Paul writes to the Church, "so account of us as ministers, servants of Christ." As ministers and servants of God we are not our own, but are brought with a price. I know some regard us as ministers of the church because the church gives us a stipend, and by doing so expect us to embellish the Gospel to fit their level of commitment. When you are a servant of the church and not Christ, the church, in some way, becomes your paymaster and its officers (deacons or board members) regard you as a subordinate and expect you to minister according to their expectations. Any minister who yields in any degree, to the expectations of church officials that do not line up with the Divine Will of God is not, in the truest sense, a minister of Christ. True servants of God will illuminate the character of a living epistle.

As servants of Christ, steward of the Gospel and mysteries of God, we are responsible for the unfolding and dispensing of God's hidden wisdom to all who will submit to His Divine Will. We are not called to please ourselves but, in accordance with the Word of God, to serve others; we must concern ourselves with, above all things, what God has purposed for us. Paul clearly lays out for believers, the foundation of their call.

> *We then that are strong ought to bear the infirmities of the weak, and not to please ourselves. ²Let every one of us please his neighbor for his good to edification. ³For even Christ pleased not himself; but, as it is written, <u>The</u> reproaches of them that reproached thee fell on me. ⁴For whatsoever things were written aforetime were written for our learning, that we through patience and comfort of the Scriptures might have hope. ⁵Now the God of patience and consolation grant you to be likeminded one toward another according to Christ Jesus:*

> ⁶*that ye may with one mind and one mouth glorify God, even the Father of our Lord Jesus Christ.*
>
> *Romans 15:1-6*

Paul writes to the Philippians, don't be dismayed at what it looks like or what appears to be the more popular opinion; there is no dishonor in being a servant:

> *If there be therefore any consolation in Christ, if any comfort of love, if any fellowship of the Spirit, if any bowels and mercies, ²fulfil ye my joy, that ye be likeminded, having the same love, being of one accord, of one mind. ³Let nothing be done through strife or vainglory; but in lowliness of mind let each esteem other better than themselves. ⁴Look not every man on his own things, but every man also on the things of others. ⁵Let this mind be in you, which was also in Christ Jesus: ⁶who, being in the form of God, thought it not robbery to be equal with God: ⁷but made himself of no reputation, and took upon him the form of a servant, and was made in the likeness of men: ⁸and being found in fashion as a man, he humbled himself, and became obedient unto death, even the death of the cross.*
>
> *Philippians 2:8*

In Matthews 20:26-28 There is a story in which a request is made by the mother of Zeb'edee's children to have her sons sit on the right and left hand of Jesus; this request angered the disciples, but Jesus said to them, don't be dismayed, this woman is of the Gentiles, of the world, of the flesh. This woman was only concerned with the welfare of her children; her request was based upon her associations, her connections, her attachments; she was functioning in a carnal environment where the princes (leaders) exercised authority over the people. He said, *but you are not of this world*; "*we are in the world but not of the world;*" as believers, elevation is not a prerequisite of our function; the greatest among us are to be the least, the servant, the minster, the under-rower (the huperetes).

How often in ministry do we see the quest for promotion supersede the willingness to serve, or the carnal security of one's welfare place above the predestined will of God. The servant always puts the concerns of the master before those of his own; when station or elevation take president over stewardship, vision is held hostage by the disposition of unworthy stewardship, the growth and development of new converts is hindered, and vision is delayed. When we see unworthy stewards prosper, it does not mean that God has given the unjust power over the believer, but in some cases God uses the unjust to prepare the just for Divine Purpose; as ministers; our Divine Purpose is tied to our walk of faith and our ability to endure hardness as good soldiers.

The underrower must be physically strong, mentally awake, and willing to obey God at any cost; he or she must be able to, by faith, see the vision from the perspective of a servant, hear the commands of the visionary (directly or through an intercessor) while at the same time remain steadfast and unmovable, compelling men for the cause of Christ; we are not to be dismayed when men don't believe us, a favorable response is not a prerequisite for stewardship; we are to sow and plant. *One man watereth, another planteth, but God gives the increase (1* **Corinthians 3;7)**. As underrowers we face carnal men with carnal ambitions and conformed characters; they do not comprehend the commitment of the servant whose life and will is that of the visionary; *we are not our own, and are bought with a price (1 Corinthians 6:20).*

It is important for the believer to think of himself as a servant, a subordinate, one whose own will is of less importance than that of his master; one whose character reflects the willingness to bear the infirmities of others. The servant seeks only to please and glorify the master (God) in all that it does. A study of the scripture will reveal that the servant's character is reflected in his or her service to God; the servant is a giver, "walking with him that ask you to walk a mile, two miles, and giving to him that ask for your coat, your cloak also.

> *And if any man will sue thee at the law, and take away thy coat, let him have thy cloke also. [41]And whosoever shall compel thee to go a mile, go with him twain*
>
> *Matthews 5:40:41*

The title "servant" is given to believers in many religious groups; believers are generally thought to be pious and steadfast in their faith and commitment. In some faiths the designation of a servant varies in importance at different levels of devotion, such as in the Catholic Church, the term "Servant of God" is a title given to those who are being considered for the office of Pope while the term "servant" in the Protestant church" refers to the faithful, the underrower, such as the altar boy or deacon, or mother of the church and should not be confused with the Servant of God as define by the Catholic Church. The expression "servant of God" appears seven times in the Bible. All four times in the old testament, (and one of the three times in the new testament,) it refers to "Moses the servant of God" (Chronicles 6:49; 2 Chronicles24:9; Nehemiah 10:29; Daniel 9:11; Revelation 15:3). In the New Testament, Paul calls himself "a servant of God" in Titus 1:1, and James calls himself "a servant of God" in James1:1 ("The servant is not greater than his lord.").

The attributes of the servant are developed through a process of commitments, dedications, and devotions; one does not automatically become a service of God; it is not an office of appointment nor is it a position of enslavement, but the true servant of God commits to the fulfillment of God's will through the teachings of Jesus Christ. He or she has resolved to endure the cross as a good soldier; the servant exemplifies the characteristic found in the fruit of the spirit, found in the Galatians 5:21.

Think for a moment of why was Moses called the "Servant of God?"

He knew God from his experience with God; He was obedient to God (even when he doubted his own ability); remember, God care little about our ability or our inabilities; He care only about our availability.

He was prayerful and courageous, steadfast and unmovable; he could have given up at any time during the journey, but he remained faithful to his charge by God as leader of His people.

SERVANT LEADERSHIP

Servant-leadership is a phrase or term coined by Robert K. Greenleaf; in his essay he states that the servant leader is servant first; this is not a new concept to committed believers. Jesus is the perfect example of the servant-leader, and like Jesus, servant-leaders are visionaries; they allow their followers to work toward achieving a common goal while encouraging others. They teach and demonstrate the presence and development of the fruit of the spirit.

Matthews 10:2-4 gives a clear picture the power Jesus had to attract followers of different stations, persuasions, personalities, characters and backgrounds who were willing to commit to his teaching, "that the Kingdom of God is at hand." We are not lords over God's heritage, but as leaders we are stewards over another's possession. Jesus, although God in the flesh, always exalted His father, never exalting Himself; He only spoke of Himself as the messenger who came to "do the will of Him that sent me".

The servant-leader must have a servant's heart; a heart of compassion, understanding and the insight to help the needy even when they cannot reach out and ask for help themselves. A servant's heart must be humble; not only humble enough to be a blessing to others, but humble enough to receive blessing. Too often does the giver feel above being given to; or the minister above being ministered to; Paul, in his letter to the church at Rome told them of his longing to visit with them and to share with them the blessings of God through ministry; he also encouraged them by telling them that he looked forward to them ministering to him, and although circumstances had kept them apart, he knew that God would someday bring it to past. As believers, if we remain humble and let the Lord take precedent over our circumstances, our emotions, our finances, and our vision, He would make a way for us to accomplish our hearts' desires, overcome our circumstances, and turn our visions into reality.

No matter who we are, or what we have accomplished, or what our educational status is, or who we know, if God has call us and we have the heart of a servant, He will make our visions reality. A servant's heart has more to do with his relationship with God than it has to do with his desires to be recognized for his deeds *(Alyice Edric the author of "A Servant's Heart")*. A believer with a servant's heart sees the need and fulfills it; he makes himself uncomfortable for the comfort of others, once again while exemplifying the fruit of the spirit: love, kindness, gentleness and the like.

> *But the fruit of the Spirit is love, joy, peace, longsuffering, gentleness, goodness, faith, Meekness, temperance: against such there is no law.*
>
> *Galatians 5:22-23*

Servant leaders are marked by their orientation, their knowledge of, and their willingness to do the will of God.

> *"Behold, as the eyes of servants look to the hands of their master, as the eyes of a maidservant to the hand of her mistress, so our eyes look to the LORD our God, till he has mercy upon us"*
>
> *Palms 123:2.*

As servants we must understand why we are called and what our calling is; although we may envision our expected end, enduring the process of turning vision into reality is a key characteristic of the servant-leader. The servant who fails to endure will forfeit or at least, delay the reality of his or her purpose. Conditions and circumstances proves our commitment to our calling, but do not assure its reality. What we go through as servants prepare us for stewardship as leaders. We need only to look at biblical leaders such as Abraham whose advancing age and the lack of faith in the promise associated with his destiny, endured the stress of nomadic roaming and lack of courage to be truthful under daring circumstance as he prepared to step into his calling as father of many nations. David was faced with the challenge of waiting for his appointed time to ascend upon the throne as ruler of God's people. Jonah was challenged with understanding the sovereignty of God in dealing with His people while Jeremiah enduring hardness as a good solider as he suffered because of God's people. The trying of our faith worketh patience.

> *"Count it all joy when ye fall into divers temptations; Knowing this, that the trying of your faith worketh patience. But let patience have her perfect work, that ye may be perfect and entire wanting nothing."*
>
> *James 1:2-4*

The list of patriarch who faced spiritual challenges because of circumstances can go on and on. As we grow through conditions and overcome circumstances, we become the believers we were purposed to be and ultimately, servant leaders with servant's hearts.

THE VISIONARY AND THE SERVANT

Many are called, few are chosen; not every minister, preacher, or evangelist has been called or sent as a visionary. Some are chosen to be supporters of vision. There are men who could never be elected to public office that are renowned for their support of visionary leaders. When we act according to God's leading regarding our ministry, we are more likely to be in place when it's our time to lead. Opportunity does not constitute leadership ability. One may have opportunity because of the death of a former Pastor, educational status, political connections, friendship, family ties, or economical ability. A true assessment of leaders who are elevated through ill-gotten means will be recognized by the stagnation and barrenness, and the like of spiritual development, commitment and dedication that enhances the growth of their fellowship.

A true servant of God does not focus on opportunity; his or her concern is what God has purposed in that season for him or her. As seasons change, our spiritual purpose changes; what God has for you in one season may change in the next season; what may be a season of harvest in one stage of your life may be a season of sowing in another; the focus of the servant is the vision of the visionary. The Assistant Pastors, Elders, Teachers, Deacons, Board Members are all servant underrowers. The underrower has but one job, that is to row; he does not concern himself with the reality of the vision; his trust is in the leader in whom he believes has a right relationship with God. If the underrower trust that the visionary (pastor or bishop or leader) is following the calling of God on his or her life, his blessing lay in that trust.

THE DISPOSITION OF
THE UNDERROWER

As more and more ministries develop out of our local churches, the need for MIT (ministers in training) workshops and seminars have increased; the ambition to become ministers is developing at an earlier stage of ministry in this generation of believer's than in previous generations; this is a reflection of the times in which we live; with the invention of the internet, other social media, and the accessibility to a wealth of biblical material that is designed to make preaching easy, not to mentioning the relaxing of the moral principles that governs our society; this has also lead to young men and women maturing faster at an earlier age; even in the church this has given rise to more "babies" in ministry, birthing premature strabismus visions (unfocused). They have zeal of godliness but are unable to see clearly what God has purposed for their lives; this is, in most cases, due to a lack of knowledge, training and commitment. Strabismus vision is not vision with divinely inspired purpose; it is vision that does not line up with God's Divine Will. The visionary sees the vision from more than one perspective and cannot line it up with the Word of God.

The lack of knowledge can be corrected through teaching, but "babies" in Christ need more than teaching; they need fathers; Paul says,

> *"For thought ye have ten thousand instructors in Christ, yet have ye not many Fathers; for in Christ Jesus I have begotten you through the gospel"*
>
> *1 Corinthians 4:15.*

There is a need for spiritual fathers; the Church is faced with training ministers for ministries in which they know very little about. In most ways, training leaders in ministry is the same as training leaders in any other business with some important exceptions; the MIT instructor must keep in mind that every function in ministry carries with it its own set of responsibilities. What God requires for the evangelist may not be the same requirement for the pastor or the teacher. While most businesses requirements carry with them competences and commitments; few require moral character and spiritual commitment, dedication, and devotion.

The oarsman, before he is entered in a race must be conditioned for the task of rowing; in the Church the spiritual progress of visionary reality rest upon the whole body of believers; unprepared, uncommitted and undevoted believers hinder the fulfillment of visionary purpose. As in the secular world, preparation for ministry is a key responsibility of leadership. One does not build a house without counting up the cost; commitment to fasting and prayer is the foundation upon which successful ministries are built; Paul admonishes us to "pray without ceasing" and to "study to show thou self-approved." Committing to memory the scripture is a requirement; it enables us to pray the scripture; David said, *"thou Word have I hidden in my heart" Psalm 119:11.* The underrower must be a scholar of the Word of God; it is the Word that reveals to us God's predestined will. We must be diligent in our effort to discharge our duties and in ministering of the Gospel. As believers we must never forget the purpose for which we are called; it is not to please men, but to draw them; such a responsibility requires that the character of the believer be without reproach; Christian character is developed by allowing the Holy Spirit to take rule over our lives and by the study of God's Word. It is a reflection of the attitudes that make up our personality and a collection of the moral fibers and dispositions that shapes our integrity. It encapsulates the full operation of the fruit of the Spirit within us.

As leaders in ministry, and underrowers for the cause of Christ we must be diligent in our study of God's Word; Paul, speaking of the Bereans said, *"they received the word with great eagerness and examined the scripture daily" Acts 17:11.* Personal study of the scripture is always notable, but whenever possible a formal Christian education should be pursued. *"My people are destroyed for the lack of knowledge" Hosea 4:6*; the priestly underrowers, pastors and other Levites are responsible for the impartation of "truth", the knowledge of God which is the light of the soul that leads to eternal life. Those who are without knowledge must not be awarded priestly elevations.

> *"I will also reject thee, that thou shalt be no priest to me:"Hosea 4;6; ill-equipped leaders are a danger to the cause of Christ. Isaiah declared that "the people are gone into captivity because they have no knowledge." Isaiah 6:13; knowledge comes through hearing (faith); but, "how can they hear with a preacher and how can he preach except he be sent.*
>
> *Romans 10:14.*

AVAILABILITY

Our walk with God should be so that He could call upon us at any time to do His bidding. God does not always give prior notice as to when He will use us; he simply creates a situation or circumstance that requires our stewardship; being ready is one of the responsibilities of the believer.

"Be ye also ready;" here Matthews speaks of a readiness to meet a soon coming king; likewise, we must also be readily prepared to do the will of God, ready to serve. Timothy said in chapter 2, that in a great house there are many vessels; some are faithful and gifted while other are gifted and unfaithful; it is with the gifted and unfaith from which most conflict in ministry arises.

> "Now in a great house there are not only vessels of gold and silver but also of wood and clay, some for honorable use, some for dishonorable. Therefore, if anyone cleanses himself from what is dishonorable, he will be a vessel for honorable use, set apart as holy, useful to the master of the house, ready for every good work."
>
> 1 Timothy 2:20-21

Readiness also includes worthiness; it is not enough to be available to do the work of God; we must also be prepared for the call to ministry; this preparation includes physical and mental as well as spiritual ability; a believer may not have the knowledge required to evangelize a city, but if he or she has a teachable spirit with which one can learn what is required to change lives for the cause of Christ, it will go a long ways in the preparation process. Giftedness sometimes hinders availability; one's gift may lead to paths outside of God's purpose and make one unavailable for a season. God does not begin by asking our ability, He ask only our availability, and if we prove our dependability, He will increase our capability. Availability also includes accessibility; worldly accessibility increases the temptation of putting trust in carnal resources; we cannot be tempted by or attracted to things to which we have no accessibility. Too many times have our interest in the carnal accessibility of things prevented us from developing total dependence upon God.

David (Psalm 20:7) warns us of those who trust in things, the physical; they will be overcome by them and in doing so will neglect to render to God their total dependence on Him; he declared *"But we remember the name of the Lord our God,"* not just the names by which God is called, such as Elohim, Elshaddai, Jehovah, and the like, although each of these names are worthy of remembrance, and emphatically serve to encourage faith in God, but here David speaks of the perfections of God, such as the goodness, wisdom, and the power of God in which we are to put our confidence.

Moses was available, assessable, and dependable, but doubted his capability; sometimes we must press beyond what we perceive to be a hindrance as to our ability and seek to make reality of what is revealed to us spiritually. Vision not only has the power to push us beyond our current reality but to also move us toward the fulfillment of our visionary purpose. This is not an overnight process; it requires determination, commitment, dedication and devotion. The enemy will test our willingness to be steadfast through a process of failures; this is done to see if we have a mind to pursue the vision set by God as our purpose, or will we just give up. Faith in God makes a difference.

Faith is trust in God when all else fails and when the natural man says otherwise. Faith looks beyond obscurity and hopelessness and sees the reality of purpose. Mature Christians stand firmly on the promises of God and are not move by winds of adversity. We may argue with God and make excuses why we feel incapable of fulfilling our call to purpose; God may allow us to use other resources (Moses used Aaron) to fulfill our call, but in the end, as with Moses, we will be the vessel He ultimately uses to get the job done; therefore, don't waste time worrying about whether or not you can do what God has told you to do or to go where He has sent you, just increase your dependability and God will make sure of your capability.

Consider the call of Gideon; when God first approached him hidden behind the winepress, He call him a "mighty man of valour," God sees beyond the personal assessment we have of ourselves and sees His predestined purpose for our lives.

> *And the angel of the LORD appeared unto him, and said unto him, The LORD is with thee, thou mighty man of valour.*
>
> *Judges 12:6*

The list of dependable vessels that were transformed into mighty men of destiny grows as we read through the scripture: David as a boy, called to be King (I Samuel 16); Esther, a slave girl, put in position to facilitate Israel's deliverance (Esther 3); Elisha, a farmer, called to be a prophet (I Kings 19:19); Let's not forget the fishermen, the persecutor, the tax collector and the doubter who were called to be apostles. It really doesn't matter whether the task to which God calls us is large or small, or whether we feel close to God or far from Him in your relationship according to his will; what really matters is our attitude of submissiveness to His divine purpose for us. As believers we know what it means to be summonsed to do the work of the Kingdom of God, and as mature Christians we ought not to question God's purpose for us; we should rather expect it. Note the attitude of Elisha when Elijah unexpectedly shows up in the field where he was plowing: Elijah shows up, takes his mantle and puts it around the shoulders of Elisha; Elisha did not question Elijah, he knew what it meant to be given the mantle of a higher authority.

Mantles were typically made of animal hair and were generally worn by kings and prophets. They were symbolic of the owners calling, position, and authority. So Elisha didn't have to ask Elijah what was going on.

He knew this was the passing of Elijah's divine calling and prophetic disposition onto him. He immediately killed his oxen, burned his plows as a symbol of his commitment to the call and his readiness to go on from there and never to go back to his past life. The question then is, how far do you want to go, and what are you willing to do to be available for your call as a servant of God?

THE SACRIFICE

We are now living in a time of spiritual prosperity where preaching, teaching, prophesying, and ministering to the needy, the sick, and the poor is in abundance; never before have we had access to so many workshops, seminars, conferences and impartations as we have today. The number of churches, ministries and faith based organizations far outnumber what we have ever had. There has been an increase in the number of religious leaders and support ministries throughout the world. World evangelism flourishes because of religious freedoms and toleration.

We do not give credit, as much as we should, to the sacrifices made by early church leaders during that seasons of ministry before we had accessibility to this season of media ministry's flourishing prosperity (television, radio, webinar, live streaming, and the like); we should not forget the time when the Church and its leaders had to endure overwhelming degrees of sacrifice to foster growth, development, and survival. As we look around today, we can't but wonder, "What happened to the church's sense of sacrifice?" As a body of believers, we collectively want the Church to be strong, highly anointed, and demonstrating the operation of the five-fold ministries. We want sound doctrine, prophetic impartations, physical growth, and financial security; yet, so very few are willing to make the sacrifices need to facilitate these graces in ministry. We are not casting any blame, but we are concerned with the image that the Church has developed over the past few decades.

Leadership in ministry requires sacrifice, and with sacrifice vision can be turned into reality. Yes, it's good to have prosperity and prophetic impartation, but it is the responsibility of leadership to try the spirits of the preachers and prophets who are allowed to speak over the lives of the sheepfold. What the Church needs more than prophecy of prosperity is the teaching of sound doctrine and a return to the principles of the doctrine: confession, repentance, and the indwelling of the Holy Spirit or should I say the Holy Ghost. It needs preachers who will preach and prophecy of what God is able to do with wretched lives in this time and season. Preacher who will preach of the power of being obedient to God's Word, and of the sacrifices needed to fulfill ones calling when he or she steps into God's Divine Purpose. I challenge the leaders and the members of their congregations to research the sacrifices that were so prevalent in the Church four or five decades ago and see where they can facilitate change in their perception of the Church of today. If we, as leaders make sure that the local church leadership (auxiliaries heads, deacons, board members) make the sacrifices needed to foster strong personal ministry development and physical ministry security, it will set the example of sacrifice for the entire congregation; then we may just see the change we're hoping to see.

Sacrifice begins with giving; first of yourself and then of your substance; God calls us to stewardship through His Word then by his servants. Our hearts must be in our stewardship; we must be passionate about our responsibility to our call to purpose. Passionate leaders and stewards persevere in times of difficulty and when challenged to be steadfast and unmovable; storms do not stop them from overcoming trials and test that are designed to destroy their visionary purpose. We are asked to "Present ourselves as living sacrifices, Holy and acceptable" for it is the least we can do. Secondly, He asked of our substance; a tithe, an offer, and gifts; our treasures belong to God "For where your treasure is, there your heart will be also" (Matthew 6:21).

VISIONARY PURPOSE

Just what is visionary purpose? Let's start by determining that God has mandated Divine Purpose for our lives; and with purpose, comes a willingness to fulfill that purpose by trusting in God. Purpose will lay barren on fallow ground if the visionary fails to submit to the voice of God. Vision is tied to and intertwined with purpose; if the visionary fails to understand his or her purpose, how then can the vision be turned into reality. According to Habakkuk, vision must be made plain and written down; the source of it (Divine inspiration) must be trusted to bring it to past.

The visionary is characterized by his or her ability to look at what is seemingly not workable or possible or practical or even idealistic and envision it as reality. Vision is one of the most powerful aspects of ministry; it stimulates action; the action of one leader multiplied by the action of the congregation can redirect the mission of a church and an organization.

Many Christians go through most of their Christian lives without developing a real sense of visionary purpose or without having a clear picture of where they are going as baptized believers. The visionary leader has the arduous responsibility of inspiring the congregation (his or her followers) to develop personal ministries that line up with the vision of the church while at the same time fulfill God's Divine Calling for their lives. The Prophet Amos (8:11-13) prophesied of a day when there would be a lack of vision and spiritual impartation because of the sins of the people and that God would remove spiritual unction from the hearts of the people; however, in today's Church there is more than enough spiritual impartation from which believers can develop unction that leads to vision, and too little application of the principles of the doctrine. There will always be those in our congregation who are not kingdom builders and thus not a part of "The Church"; the sum total of their Christian experience is their association with the physical church; as important as the physical church may seem, it is the development of our spiritual house that pleases God the most. All visionaries are not leaders; some are chosen to be subordinate supporters of vision. The fivefold ministry is a good example of how individual callings in ministry work together for the fulfilling of divinely inspired vision; the Apostle governs, the Evangelist gathers, the Pastor guards, the Prophet guides, and the Teacher grounds. Each of these ministries may be the calling of different individuals, but all for the perfecting of the Church, while at the same time, they demonstrate support for the Divine Purpose that God had placed on the visionary leaders (Pastors).

Discernment is one of the more important gifts that the visionary leaders can possess; it ensures that the impartations of other visionaries (those who come to help) and connect themselves to their vision and that they are divinely inspired. Like the Pastor, the subordinate leader has the same responsibility of understanding the purpose of his or her calling. Title or office does not constitute calling; visionary leaders must try the spirit of those who desire to attach themselves to their divine purpose. It is not enough to trust the resume or trust the biography of an enthusiastic supporter along. Gideon made sure it was God who promised to give him victory over the Midianites, and like Gideon we must make sure of those who come to connect themselves to our vision.

> *Beloved, believe not every spirit, but try the spirits whether they are of God: because many false prophets are gone out into the world. ² Hereby know ye the Spirit of God: Every spirit that confesseth that Jesus Christ is come in the flesh is of God: And every spirit that confesseth not that Jesus Christ is come in the flesh is not of God: and this is that spirit of antichrist, whereof ye have heard that it should come; and even now already is it in the world. ⁴ Ye are of God, little children, and have overcome them: because greater is he that is in you, than he that is in the world*
>
> *1 John 4:1-5*

When the visionary leader turns key elements of his or her vision over to those who connect themselves to them without trying their spirits or discernment their purpose or determine whether their proclaim to have divine unction or spiritual inclination is real, he or she risk delaying the reality of his or her predestined purpose. Moses, in Deuteronomy, listened to the voice of the congregation over that of God who had commanded that he lead the children of Israel over Jordan into the Promised Land; this delayed the promise for more than 40 years. The visionary must, at all cost, resolve to obey the voice of God regardless of the circumstances.

Jehoshaphat, faced with insurmountable odds (2 Chronicles 20:1-30) did not turn to the people for advice when the enemy was approaching; he knew where his help lay; he reminded God of the promises He made to Israel regarding the Promise Land; then he required that the people, along with himself, seek God's help for deliverance. God, responding to their cry, sent an answer by the prophet Jahaziel and said, "tell the people to not be afraid, God will deliver them;" Jehoshaphat was determined to trust and obey God because the enemy was much greater and more experience in warfare than Israel.

FROM CURRENT REALITY TO VISIONARY PURPOSE

Current reality is seeing yourself where you are; there is a danger in connecting to what we consider current reality; we should take assessment of the "Now," and evaluate what brought us to our current station in life. The visionary must never be satisfied with things the way they are; there is a danger of creating a comfort zone that hinders the process of turning vision into reality. It is in the "now" that we associate, evaluate, perceive, and decide as it relates to the future; it is in this stage of ministry where the enemy attacks our spiritual inclinations, but in spite of what it looks like, we must stand on the promises of God. In the 'now" the visionary must define current reality, identify its weaknesses and shortcomings then make known what he or she sees as the unction that the Holy Spirit has divinely purposed.

Speaking of purpose and visionary unction is just the beginning of the visionary's work; James has admonished us to "be doers of the word." How many times have we heard ministers, or should I say people plan to do something, but never get around to doing what has been laid on their hearts to do? Speaking positively of where God has purposed you to go is part of the process of turning current reality and into visionary purpose. Affirmations must be made and made in the present tense such as: "I am, it is, I will, God has;" hearing of your resolve is a good way to keep what God has put in your heart afresh: "I can do all thing through Christ Jesus who strengthens me," "No weapon that forms against me shall proper," "lean not to thin own understanding, but in all thou way acknowledge him and he will direct you path." Affirmation like these will helps keep us focus on our vision.

We are bound to encounter some failure in our quest to turn vision into reality; we must not expect to succeed in every effort we put forth. God uses failure and disenchantment to try our steadfastness and our total dependence on Him. Remember, "The trying of your faith is much more precious" than that of silver and gold, or any other material substance that we may obtain. "If need be, ye are in heaviness through manifold temptations;" the test of one visionary may not be the test of another; we must not expect our visionary reality to be as easily attainable as the pastors down the street; nor should we expect that our trial will be as server, but we must "earnestly contend for the faith which was once delivered unto the saints" Jude 1:3. There are those who have been assigned to try our worthiness to attain God's blessings of Grace.

The seeds of all behavior are planted (stored) in the neuron section of our brain, good and bad; the flesh is gratified by our desires; our desires are formulated according to the development of our faith and dependence on God. The more we trust and depend on the Lord, the less likely the seeds of the adversary will flourish. By allowing the Lord to take president over our lives, we turn over our fallow ground and uproot the seeds of adversity that are designed to choke and kill our visionary reality. Purpose must be nurtured and not allowed to lay barren.

I was working in my garden when I noticed several things about growth and development; when I planted the seeds, they all did not come up at the same time, but eventually most of them came up. Some never came up; although they were in the same plot of ground and received the same care; "many are called, few are chosen." Some plants grew strong and tall and produced much fruit, others produced an average amount while a few produced a disappointing amount. Even in the strongest plant which produced nice big juicy fruit, there were some fruit that just didn't develop. I noticed that in a bean pod there would be five or six beautiful beans, but in the middle of the pod, between two beautifully developed bean there would be one that did not develop at all.

We are all working in one church, under one visionary, inspired by the same spirit; yet some will not develop to the same level of ministry; some will be moved by inclination and ambition; others will be move by the divine providence of God; some will be move by academia and opportunity. We all know individuals in ministry who fit into one of the aforementioned situations. This is not to say that a believer should not seek to move to the next level in ministry, but if a man strive to be elevated (for masteries) let him strive lawfully *2 Timothy 2:5*

The Apostle infers that to strive lawfully may entail spiritual warfare; he infers when we are presented with that opportunity to do thing the right way, the enemy often presents another way, perhaps an easier way or a shorter way. "When I desired to do good, evil was there."

PRAYERS OF THE UNDERROWER

Prayer during the time of Jesus was a daily requirement under the law. Some believers, like the hypocrites who prayed standing in the synagogues, prayed to be seen; there was no reward in their prayers; they prayed because it was an obligation or tradition, but Jesus, in Matthew 6:5-15 begins his instruction on prayer with a correction in regards to "how to pray". Some Jews knew prayer only as a tradition. Jesus inferred that prayer should be more about the one praying than the one to whom the prayer is offered. He simply says, some who claim to be believers are not praying sincerely but are simply "play acting" the role of a believer. As leaders in the Lord's Church we are admonished to know them that labor among us and to try ever spirit by the Word.

Prayer connects us with God; no amount of good that you do can connect you to God the way prayer can; remember the ruler who said, "I have kept the commandments" or I have been a good man since my youth, shouldn't that have some barring on his relationship with God? No, what good is a radio if it is not connected to a server or an electric fan on a hot day if it is not connect to an electric output. Pray is the believer's secret weapon; one cannot develop into an underrower without a strong prayer life. Learning to be an underrower is a process. Believers have to grow into maturity as Christians before they can endure the hardship or embrace the responsibility of underrowing. New believers are called "babies" in the scripture; they develop into mature Christians by eating what is called the "sincerer milk of the Word." After becoming more mature there is a process that one must go through (Studying, fasting, praying, enduring sound doctrine, even giving up right for wrong). All these things help make believers into strong underrowers. The underrower must learn how to trust God, to trust leadership, to stand on the promises of God, and to use the scripture as a weapon against Satan.

Prayer is what gives the underrower the grace to serve; it fosters the liberty to serve without merit or for payment. Prayer is an amazing weapon against the wiles of the devil: pride, unfaithfulness, intemperance, impatience, and all that makes a believer focus on or accept anything other than the will of God; it is the believers weapon against anything detrimental to the believer's growth and development as visionaries. Prayer sustain us when we are in our fiery furnace or our lion's dens; it gives us strength amid our trials and when we feel like giving up.

Prayer is not just the house in which we live, it is the foundation upon which our lives are built. Our prayer life cannot just be a footer (that which is dug a few feet down and is designed to sustain a limited structure), but prayer must be built on a strong foundation, a foundation that is able to holdup the heaviest of our trial, and the most difficult of our struggles, the most challenging of the wiles of the devil.

Prayer must sustain the believer physically, emotionally, economically, personally, physiologically, and monetarily in every area of our lives as believers, it must sustain us. We can pray for the enlargement of the scope of ministry, or for more enlightenment of our visionary purpose, or for the strengthening of our faith, or for the development of our Christian character; nothing is out of the bounds of prayer. Man should always pray; it should be as natural to the believer as walking and talking. We should study the scripture on prayer and commit them to memory.

> *Watch and pray, that ye enter not into temptation: the spirit indeed is willing, but the flesh is weak.*
>
> *Matt 26:41 KJV*

> *And this I pray, that your love may abound yet more and more in knowledge and in all judgment;*
>
> *Phil 1:9 KJV*

Pray without ceasing.

Thess 5:17 KJV

The Bible is complete with examples of how prayer brought believers out of situations beyond their own power: The Hebrew boys, Daniel, David, the blind man, the women with the issue of blood and so on. Each of these incidents call for sincerity and total dependence on God.

There are believers in places where they do not have access to medical, social, or governmental assistance to help them in their times of adversity; their only option is total dependence God through prayer; here, in America, believers have so many options that they tend to trust in these options rather than God, but where there are fewer options prayer is the key to deliverance. Prayer is more powerful than a locomotive, faster and a speeding pullet; those were metaphors used in the fifties and sixties; today we would use metaphors such as frequency and the speed of light, the power of the adam.

As you develop your prayer life, make sure your worship is for real and there is fervency in your connection with God, otherwise your prayer is only the utterance of a collection of eclectic papery (word).

THE WEAPON OF OUR WARFARE

Put on the whole armour of God, that ye may be able to stand against the wiles of the devil.

For we wrestle not against flesh and blood, but against principalities, against powers, against the rulers of the darkness of this world, against spiritual wickedness in high places.

Wherefore take unto you the whole armour of God, that ye may be able to withstand in the evil day, and having done all, to stand.

Ephesians 6:11-13

(For the weapons of our warfare are not carnal, but mighty through God to the pulling down of strong holds;) Casting down imaginations, and every high thing that exalteth itself against the knowledge of God, and bringing into captivity every thought to the obedience of Christ;

2 Corinthians 10:4-5 KJV

"They are not carnal, but mighty to God to the pulling down of strongholds." We previously referred to prayer as "the life of a repentant heart," it is also the weapon most used by the believer to fight against the wiles of the Devil. Songs move people, good preach inspire congregations, good sermons help develop ministries, but prayer moves God.

If you want to move God, send up a fervent prayer; prayer is not a ritual of closing your eyes and putting on a holy face; you don't have to kneel down or sit, you can pray while walking along, while cooking your evening dinner, or while going about your daily duties. God response to the sincerity of prayer, not to the utterance of beauty words, not to the well-crafted phrases. It is our most needed weapon when fighting against the powers of this world.

Let's not underestimate the power of principalities and spiritual weaknesses. We must look at these two imposters from two perspectives: the natural and the spiritual; naturally, a principality is a territory ruled by a prince or some governmental authority; spiritual weakness in high places is often referred to as those who are in authority but fail to hear God or follow His commands. These individuals are usually ruled by Satan. Thus, whatever he wants them to do, he has the power to influence them; the men of this world who are not saved by the power of the Holy Ghost, will do it, providing God does not step in to prevent it.

Principalities refers to the vast array of evil and malicious spirits that make war against the people of God. The principalities and powers of Satan viewed in this text, are beings that exert their power in unseen realms to oppose everything and everyone that is of God. The only weapon we have is prayer, pray the scripture…. "no weapon that form against me shall prosper," "by his scrips we are healed."

Prayer changes live, opens doors, mend bridges, changes directions, strengthens relationships; no two prayers are alike; fervency make every prayer different. Although two individuals may utter the same words fervency make the difference. Prayers don't have to be long and eloquent; they need only come from a sincere and humble heart. Prayer does not fit us for the greater work; prayer is the grater work. We should pray because we believe in the power of prayer; we prayer because we have no doubt that God will answer our prayers. If you don't pray regularly you are missing out on the greatest source of power known to man.

When you pray, turn it loose; don't try to manipulate or force the outcome; just trust God to do what is right for you. Perhaps you have never prayed, don't be dismayed or disheartened; God's ears are not heavy that He cannot hear; just open your mouth a say what you want to Him;

> *This the confidence we have in approaching God that if we ask anything according to His will, he hears us*
>
> 1 John 5:14

We are created in the image of God; He desires a personal relationship with us; Although all transcending, omnipotent and sovereign God wants a personal relationship with us. He is aware of all we do, present with us at all time, and compassionately involved in every aspect of our lives. There is no secret of what God can and will do if we trust Him. What He has done for others, He'll do the same thing for you. Prayer putts us all a the same playing field with God. There is no big "i's" an little "you's" when it comes to God hearing our prayers.

www.ingramcontent.com/pod-product-compliance
Lightning Source LLC
Chambersburg PA
CBHW021451070526
44577CB00002B/350